NATURE'S NURSERIES

"Eyes and No Eyes" Series

by Arabella B. Buckley

- I. Wild Life in Woods and Fields
- II. By Pond and River
- III. Plant Life in Field and Garden
- IV. Birds of the Air
- V. Trees and Shrubs
- VI. Insect Life

by R. Cadwallader Smith

- VII. On the Seashore
- VIII. Within the Deep
- IX. Riverside Rambles
- X. Highways and Hedgerows
- XI. Nature's Nurseries
- XII. O'er Moor and Fen

"EYES AND NO EYES" SERIES   BOOK XI

NATURE'S NURSERIES

BY

R. CADWALLADER SMITH

YESTERDAY'S CLASSICS
ITHACA, NEW YORK

Cover and arrangement © 2020 Yesterday's Classics, LLC.

This edition, first published in 2020 by Yesterday's Classics, an imprint of Yesterday's Classics, LLC, is an unabridged republication of the text originally published by Cassell and Company, Ltd. For the complete listing of the books that are published by Yesterday's Classics, please visit www.yesterdaysclassics.com. Yesterday's Classics is the publishing arm of Gateway to the Classics which presents the complete text of hundreds of classic books for children at www.gatewaytotheclassics.com.

ISBN: 978-1-63334-119-7

Yesterday's Classics, LLC
PO Box 339
Ithaca, NY 14851

CONTENTS

I. Fish Families 1

II. Froggie's Family 8

III. The Insect Nursery 15

IV. Nurseries in Birdland 22

V. Nurseries in Birdland
(continued) 29

VI. Meal-Time in Birdland 36

VII. Lesson-Time in Birdland 44

VIII. The Babes in the Wood. 50

IX. The Babes in the Wood
(continued) 58

X. Beware of the Enemy! 65

XI. Playtime 70

XII. Playtime
(continued) 75

CHAPTER I

FISH FAMILIES

Baby fish, like baby frogs, when they first see the world are quite unlike their parents. The sea swarms with countless numbers of these fish-babies: if you scooped up some of them in a bucket, you would hardly know that they were fish. But let us begin at the beginning—the egg!

A bird's egg, as we all know, is a hard shell containing "white" and yolk. Is that all? No, we have left out the most important part, called the *germ*. The chick is formed neither from the yolk nor the "white," but from a minute "germ." This is a speck of life, but, by living on the large yellow yolk, and the transparent "white," it grows and grows, and by slow degrees becomes a perfect chick. The yolk is so large, and is such rich food, that it lasts until the chick is perfectly formed and ready to burst through the hard walls of its prison.

The baby fish is not so well off. It comes out of a tiny egg, in which is no room for a rich store of food for the *germ* to live on. So, of course, it cannot wait within the egg until it is a perfect fish, but must come out and face the world as an imperfect one. In this baby form it is known as a *larval* fish.

The bird baby is well off, for, on leaving the egg, it is a small copy of its parents, while the fish or frog, coming from a starved little egg, is merely a *larva*. It has to become a perfect fish or frog *outside* the shelter of the egg! We might compare it with the child of poor parents, forced to go into the big world before it has really grown up!

Frogs' eggs are easy to keep: most of us have watched them hatch into tadpoles, and the tadpoles develop into small frogs. But fish-eggs are more difficult to keep: so let us suppose we have dived into the clear water of a sparkling stream where we can see the eggs of a trout. They were laid in the clean gravel bed, several hundred of them, nearly three months ago! Although the fish did her best to cover them over with gravel, many have been gobbled up by ducks, eels, and other enemies; but those that escaped are now ready to hatch.

Each egg breaks, and out wriggles a queer little object with two black discs on its head—its eyes. Can this odd-looking scrap of life ever become a handsome, strong, speckled trout? As it lies on its side, tired out with the exertion of escaping from prison, we notice a queer lump fastened to the underside of its body. What can it be?

It is a part of the egg-yolk; and for the next few

weeks the baby fish depends on it for food. If you like, you can call it the baby's feeding-bottle. Only, as you will notice in our picture *(below)*, the feeding-bottle is not connected with the baby's mouth, but with its body! Why is that?

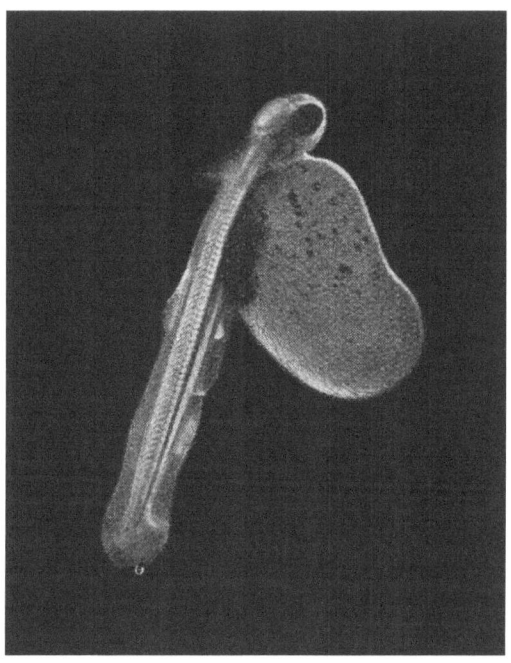

TROUT ALEVIN

WHEN FIRST HATCHED, TROUT ARE KNOWN AS "ALEVIN."

The reason is a strange one. The throat, or food-pipe, is at first closed up, therefore the baby would starve and die, but for the remains of egg-yolk in the "feeding-bottle." This store of food keeps the little creature alive, and it can stay hidden away in the gravel while it is so weak and helpless.

NATURE'S NURSERIES

So the weeks go by: our baby fish escapes its many enemies, comes out of hiding, and we see it chasing and eating small things, such as water-fleas. Its food-bag has now all gone. It begins to look more like a fish. It has a good appetite for small worms, grubs, and fresh-water shrimps, and so grows up to be a lovely, shining, red-spotted Trout.

Now all fish do not begin life quite in that way, but a great many do. As the eggs and babies have no nursery, and no parents to protect them, many are destroyed; to make up for this, each female fish must lay a great number of eggs. Some of our river-fish lay many, but sea-fish take first prize for huge families. The Cod, for instance, lays millions of eggs, the Flounder more than 1,000,000, and the Herring from 20,000 to 40,000!

The Herring, Cod, and most of the fish you see in the fish-shop, are very careless parents. They simply shed their *spawn* into the sea, and swim away as if nothing had happened! We must notice, however, that they do not lay their eggs just *anywhere* in the great ocean, but in certain parts. They choose suitable water, neither too cold nor too warm, neither too deep nor too shallow!

This habit is a most important one—for us as well as for them. The Herring likes to shed its eggs in fairly shallow water. The Cod gather in millions off the coast of Newfoundland, where the water is perfect

FISH FAMILIES

for the eggs, the babies, and the grown-up Cod as well. Now fishermen study these habits of fish: they know when and where to find the mighty shoals of Herring as they travel to the spawning-beds: and we all know of the famous Cod-fishery of the foggy Banks of Newfoundland.

The eggs of these fish do not take months to hatch, like those of the Trout, but a few days only. When we consider the dangers they run it is surprising that so many fish remain! The shoals of Herring, for instance, are beyond count! In the year 1927 no fewer than 21 million of these fish were landed by Yarmouth fishing boats in *one day,* and the total catch for one week, at this seaport only, was 85 *million Herrings!*

All fish are not so careless of their eggs as the Herring, Cod, etc. The Trout and Salmon, for instance, hide them under gravel: others do more than this, and make nests: and some, like our common Stickleback, or "Red-Throat" as boys call him, even guard their eggs and young. Most of us have seen how fiercely this handsome little fellow guards his property. How he makes brave charges at intruders, with spines set like fixed bayonets. He is ready to fight anyone and everyone; in his Spring suit of green and red and gold, he shines like a jewel against the mud of his watery home.

Scattered all over the world are other nest-building fish: and, like the birds, each has its own idea of the best kind of nest to make. Strange to say, there

NATURE'S NURSERIES

are fish which have a special pocket of skin in which to carry the eggs. The common Pipe-fish (which you may see at the Zoo, or sometimes at the fish-shop, or in nets at the seaside) is one of these fish with pockets. Another queer fish, to be found in tropical seas (and also at the Zoo!) carries the eggs in its mouth and gills, until they hatch! Needless to say, this fish is content with a small family of 20 or 30.

NEST OF STICKLEBACK

Round our own coasts may be found fish which place their eggs in empty shells, and mount guard over them. Others there are which press their eggs into rock crevices, and protect them with their own bodies from roving enemies.

But fish that build nurseries, or guard their families in any way, are rare. As a rule, there is no nursery life for the baby fish. After leaving the egg, it finds itself helpless in a world of enemies. The chances are that it will soon be found by one of them, and speedily eaten!

EXERCISES

1. How does the baby trout exist for the first few weeks of its life?

2. Where do the Cod lay their eggs? Name one famous Cod fishery, and one port famous for its fleet of Herring boats.

3. Mention four fish which lay their eggs and leave them, and two which guard their eggs.

CHAPTER II

FROGGIE'S FAMILY

In early Spring-time, when "pussy-willows" are beginning to look gay, and the Marsh Marigolds flaunt their shining yellow in the swamps, Froggie journeys to the water, to lay her eggs. In a few days' time, masses of jelly, dotted with little black spots, show where she has been. But we see no sign of Froggie, for she has hidden in the grass and weeds, leaving her eggs to look after themselves.

"But all frogs do that," you may say, "and they never behave in any other way." It is quite true that our frogs never show any regard for their families. Some frogs of other lands behave in a very different way, however, as we shall see later in this lesson. First let us see the many curious things that happen to Froggie's eggs.

The frog's life is like a story with many chapters, though very few of Froggie's big family live from Chapter 1 to the end of the story! The eggs, tadpoles, and baby frogs are, to many creatures, what chocolate-cream is to boys and girls—something to be made an

FROGGIE'S FAMILY

end of at once! So the frog's family daily gets less and less! As the eggs have no protecting nursery, it is as well that the frog—like the cod and herring we saw in the last lesson—lays so many of them!

Now fishes and frogs, as you know, are not related. They belong to two distinct groups in Nature's great family, but in one thing at least they are alike. Both the baby frog, and the baby fish, when they first hatch into the world, appear in a form quite unlike that of their parents. They are, in fact, in a larval stage.

About two weeks after Froggie laid her eggs, a little black creature wriggles out of each jelly envelope, in which it has passed Chapter 1 of its life. In Chapter 2 it is very lazy. It does nothing but cling to the water-weed by means of two suckers under its head. It has no eyes and no mouth. It is simply waiting for its mouth to grow. And, as it is not really a tadpole yet, we must call it a *larva*. It breathes by means of tufts that branch from each side the "neck."

Chapter 2 ends in a few days, when our larval frog has a mouth. A very small mouth, but a strange one! It is armed with wonderful rows of rasps, or teeth. If our eyes were immensely strong, we could count more than 600 of these tiny teeth! The two beady eyes also appear now, but the breathing tufts soon disappear.

Our larva has gone a stage farther in its life-story. It has reached Chapter 3 in which it is a tadpole, breathing like a fish through slits in each side of its neck. It eats greedily, and grows. For the most part it feeds on particles of weed, but is quite ready to dine off the dead bodies of its own relations! Its body is inky black with gold spangles, and, like a fish, it swims by wriggling its strong tail.

In Chapter 4 of its story we must call it a frog-tadpole, for its legs begin to show, first the long hind ones, and then the front ones. It is leaving its baby tadpole period, and nearing the time when it will be a perfect frog. But first it has some most important changes to make, before it can enter Chapter 5 of its life, and leave the water.

The frog-tadpole ceases to feed, and casts off its gills and jaws! Other wonderful changes occur in its body: it begins now to come to the surface of the water. Perhaps you can guess the reason? It has given up breathing by means of *gills,* as a fish breathes, and now needs air to fill its *lungs,* just as we do. At last it has gone through all the stages of its babyhood, and swims ashore as a little frog. It has reached the last chapter of its life as a water-baby: if it does not now hurry ashore all the tadpoles seem to take a delight in nibbling its toes!

Before entering on its new life on land, it throws away its old clothes. In other words, it casts its skin: its tail, as you see in the picture opposite is now nearly all gone. Has it dropped off? No, it was not wasted, but used up as food by the body, during that eventful

Chapter 4, when so many things are happening to the frog-tadpole that it is unable to eat.

YOUNG FROG WITH ITS CAST SKIN

Our baby frog sets out, with thousands of others, to seek its fortune on land—only to meet more enemies! Being no larger than your finger nail, it can hide away in the daytime in any tiny crevice, coming out at night when the earth is moist. After a spell of dry weather, the first rain-storm brings the froglings out in their thousands, until the earth seems alive with them. Indeed, it used to be said that they had "all fallen down with the rain"! They set out to explore the world—much to the delight of all the ducks in that district!

We leave them to grow up into big frogs, while we skip several thousand miles in search of other frogs.

In the country of Brazil lives one which is called by the natives "The Blacksmith," for its voice resounds like the hammer on the smith's anvil. But it also has the habit of making a kind of nursery for its eggs and young.

To make the nursery, the female frog collects mud for building material, and uses her feet as a mason uses his trowel. She plasters the mud together, and so constructs a round wall in the shallow water of a pond or marsh. She works until the edges of this mud basin show above the water. She then levels the floor, lays her eggs inside the basin, and leaves them.

Another frog of the same country makes a neater nest than that. She climbs up the stem of a plant. Then, with the help of her mate, she bends a leaf into the shape of a funnel. In this odd nest she deposits her eggs, where they are fairly safe from enemies.

But there are other frogs, and toads also, which are not content with such nurseries. They make no nest at all, but prefer to carry their eggs about with them! Toads, as you may know, lay their eggs in long rows, like so many pearls in a necklace, and leave them in the water. But a foreign toad has the odd habit of winding the eggs *around his hind legs!* With this jelly string coiled about him, he hides away until night-time, when he comes out to eat and bathe the eggs in a pond or in dew. The female toad has nothing to do with them once they are laid: but Mr. Toad makes himself useful, and acts as a nurse as well as a nursery!

FROGGIE'S FAMILY

We will look at one more nursery, and that one perhaps the oddest of all! In this case we find a male frog taking charge of the eggs; and instead of placing them on his body, he thrusts them into a pouch, or bag, under his mouth! This is surely an odd place for a nursery! Of course his family is a small one—about a dozen eggs, as a rule. This frog was discovered by the great naturalist Darwin: it is also famous as being the smallest frog in the world—it never grows beyond half an inch in length!

Though the queer frogs and toads we have glanced at are dwellers in foreign lands, you may sometimes see them at the Zoo. Two things we must notice before we leave them: one is, that the *male* frog or toad is sometimes the nurse; another is, that they have *small* families, and not large ones like those of our own frogs and toads. Can you guess the reason?

EXERCISES

1. Keep some frog-spawn in a jar of water; make drawings of the eggs and tadpoles.

2. Write what you know of each chapter in the frog's life.

3. What happens to the tail of the tadpole?

4. What made some people say that the baby frogs "fell down with the rain"?

5. Describe the nursery habits of one foreign frog or toad.

CHAPTER III

THE INSECT NURSERY

CAN you think of any insects which make nurseries, or tend their young? Of course you will at once remember the hive of the wonderful honey-bee, and the nests of wasp and ant! Those three insects rear their babies with remarkable care.

In the hive, nurses attend day and night to those cells which contain eggs or *larvæ* (grubs). They bring food to the growing grub, clean out its nursery, and in every way devote themselves to their work as nurses. They act as if they knew that the health of the babies was most important for the welfare of the whole hive!

If you look into the teeming ant-town you find the same care taken. If the egg-nursery in the underground nest is too warm or too cool, at once the eggs are carried to another part of the nest. The grubs, when hatched, are quite helpless; they depend on their nurses, and would soon die if neglected. There is no fear of that! They are fed and cleaned. Is the sun shining warmly on the nest? Then up they must go for an airing. If you then open the nest what a rush and a scramble take place!

NATURE'S NURSERIES

But, even in the face of great danger, see how the ants' first care is for their young! Each ant seizes one in her jaws, and does her best to carry it to a place of safety.

Later on, the grubs become cocoons, and still they are watched and tended, and carried here and there. And when the little prisoner is ready to emerge from the cocoon, the nurses are there, eager to help. With their strong jaws they cut open the tough envelope, and assist the weak baby from its old coverings. At first it is too feeble to crawl. So they bring it food, lick it, and watch over it until it is strong enough to take its share in the work of the nest.

An insect of warm countries, the Termite or White Ant, builds nests that are as hard as the hardest cement. Only part of the nest shows above the earth; but it is so large that from a distance a number of such nests may be mistaken for a native village! The baby White Ants are kept in special nurseries in this huge insect city. (*See* coloured picture *opposite*.)

As you know, the nurses in the ant-nest and beehive are *workers*. The eggs are laid by the *queen*, who has no other duty to perform. There are, however, many kinds of bees and wasps which live alone, and not in a hive or nest. Let us follow one, and see how she provides for her young.

On a sunny bank in early summer we see a wasp-like insect, orange-and-black in colour, flying and running quickly to and fro. She is much too excited

THE INSECT NURSERY

and busy to sting you or do anything at all but rush about on her long legs. Is she looking for food? Yes, but not for herself.

NEST OF WHITE ANT

At last she dashes under a dead leaf. In a minute she is out again, dragging a fat spider as large as herself! How she tugs and tugs at that spider! If its legs catch in the grass she only pulls all the harder. It *has* to come where she wishes. Then she leaves the spider in a tuft of grass and flies away.

After a time we see the wasp return. She hunts about like a dog looking for a lost bone! Soon she finds her spider, and again pulls at it with all her strength. We follow her, and at length we watch her stop by a neat little hole in the sand. This is the end of her journey, for she drags the spider down, and out of our sight.

Perhaps you can guess the meaning of her actions! She will lay her egg on the spider: and, after filling the hole up, will fly away and return no more. Her nursery task was a hard one, was it not? Of course the egg hatches into a grub, which eats the poor spider, and in due time itself becomes a spider-hunting wasp.

Perhaps you wonder why the fierce spider does not struggle for life, and use its poison fangs. The reason is that the wasp, when she made her first attack, cleverly stung her prey so that it can no longer fight or even move!

Most insects take no notice of their eggs or young. You know how the Cabbage Butterfly, for instance, lays her eggs on a cabbage and flits gaily away in the sunshine. Nature guides her, and hosts of other insects, to lay their eggs where the young will find food; but that is all.

Now one common and despised insect may be said to act like a mother—the Earwig. In early Spring the Earwig starts her nursery duties by burrowing into the soil and laying about fifty eggs that look like little pearls. You would expect her to run away then, and

THE INSECT NURSERY

forget all about them!

Instead of doing that she remains in the hole, generally head down, to guard her eggs. Now if you scatter this odd nursery you will find that very soon the eggs are replaced and covered up by the careful insect. And, strange to say, the Earwig will sometimes move her precious eggs from one burrow to another—perhaps to a drier or warmer spot!

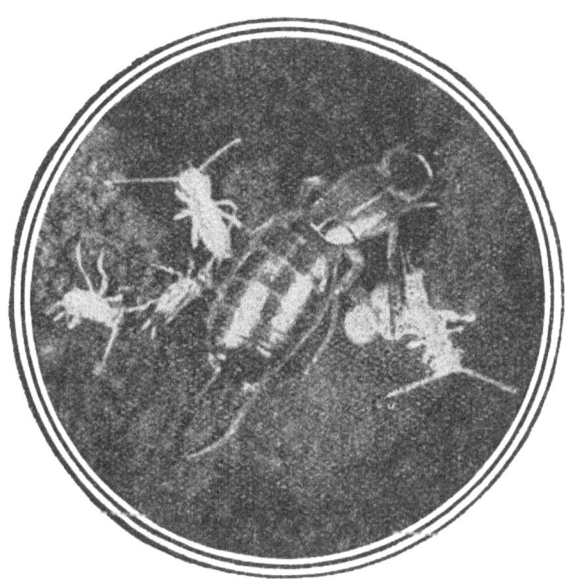

EARWIG AND YOUNG

In our picture *(above)* you see the mother Earwig with a few eggs, and some newly-hatched babies. Notice that they are much like the adult insect in shape: Earwigs do not begin life as grubs, like so many other insects. Notice, too, the silvery colour of the baby

Earwigs, making them look like little ghosts. But they are active, hungry ghosts, ready to run about and feed, though what they find to eat I cannot say. They *do* feed, however, for in two weeks' time their coats are too tight. Each one then moults—that is, it casts off its old skin.

YOUNG EARWIGS

The mother insect still guards them. She finds new feeding-places, with her brood around her. Four times the young ones cast off their old clothes. Our picture *(above)* shows you how the grown Earwig appears after casting off its skin for the last time. In an hour or two that silvery colour darkens, and the Earwig becomes a shiny brown.

By this time it has left the nursery. It is now grown-up, with short wing-cases under which are

THE INSECT NURSERY

two lovely gauzy wings folded and packed into one of the neatest of parcels! The mother Earwig has by now another nursery to watch over.

Any gardener will tell you that "The Earwig is a pest. We kill it because it eats our flowers, especially our dahlias." Now, if you could examine the Earwig after its nightly feast in your garden, what would you find? You would find in it bits of slugs, caterpillars, greenfly—all of them enemies in the garden. So perhaps the Earwig has not had a fair trial. It does some harm in the garden; it also does good, and possibly it does more good than harm! In the care of its eggs and young it is our most interesting insect. And please remember that the Earwig has not the least desire to enter your ear!

EXERCISES

1. Name four insects which tend their eggs and young.

2. Describe the way in which the Solitary Wasps provide for their young.

3. Where have you seen Earwigs? Describe one; what colour are the young Earwigs?

4. In what way is the Earwig more interesting than other insects?

CHAPTER IV
NURSERIES IN BIRDLAND

OUR carpenters, plasterers, miners and weavers all use different tools for their work. But the birds, in their plastering, weaving, mining and wood-cutting use only a pair of nippers—the beak. Some of their work you can see in our coloured pictures on pages 27, 34, and 42.

The nursery-building of the cheeky Sparrow, and of many other birds, is soon done. The Sparrow puts together an untidy mass which, perhaps, chokes a water-pipe on your house and is washed away by the first storm. Others take great pains, and construct such homes as those you see on page 27: they are woven with dry grass and fibre. These weaving birds seem to love such work, and even in captivity will weave together every straw and thread they can find. The little Tailor-bird of India makes a cup-like nursery by sewing two or three leaves together. Where does it find needle and cotton? Its bill is the needle, and a caterpillar cocoon furnishes the silk!

Our garden friends, the Tits, build in a cosy hole. Mr. Titmouse does the house-hunting: he seeks

NURSERIES IN BIRDLAND

a dry place with a very narrow entrance. He has many a journey before calling his wife to see the new home. Once they are pleased they are not easily scared away.

A pair of Blue Tits, finding nesting-sites somewhat rare, decided to start house-keeping in a letter-box. They could scarcely have chosen a worse place: but they thought otherwise, and were determined to stay there! Mr. Blue Tit claimed the letter-box as his property, and when his wife left him with eight eggs to guard, he became quite angry and hissed like a snake every time a letter was dropped in.

I expect you can mention other birds that love to hide their nests in holes. There is the little Sand Martin, which looks much too weak to be a miner! Yet he and his mate, working in turn, dig a tunnel three feet in length, loosening the sand with their beaks, and kicking it out of the burrow. They clear a larger space at the end—always above the level of the entrance, so that rain cannot enter. And here, in a nest of grass and feathers, they hatch their five or six pure white eggs.

The Green Woodpecker, and his two cousins the Greater-spotted and Lesser-spotted Woodpeckers, make holes in tree-trunks for their nursery. You will more often hear these birds than see them for they are all three skilful players at hide-and-seek. A Green Woodpecker I once watched had made a wonderfully neat hole in the trunk of an oak. Some wild bees were already nesting in the hollow of that tree, and the

Woodpecker soon had to find another nesting-site!

In the same wood a Nuthatch had stolen a hole made by a Woodpecker, and although the owner came to claim his property the Nuthatch fought with wing and beak, hissing with all his might. After winning the battle, he started to plaster up the entrance to the hole with mud and gravel—an odd habit of these birds. In this way they keep out inquisitive enemies, and also prevent the baby Nuthatches from falling out.

One of the loveliest nurseries in the world is that of the Long-tailed Tit, or Bottle Tit *(see* coloured picture, page 34). This dainty bird, common in our woods all the year round, is the weakest of all the Tit family. Perhaps that is why he does not fight for nesting-holes, but builds instead a pretty covered nursery in the open.

A tiny hole serves as entrance to this dome-shaped nest, marked very often by a curved white feather. Many birds desert their nurseries if you disturb them, but the Long-tails will not do so if you gently feel inside. How soft and cosy it is! More than 2,000 feathers have been counted in one of these nests; one by one, they had all been carried there. The walls are built of moss, wool, and spider silk, felted together, and the outside covered with lichen from tree-trunks.

Cup-shaped nurseries are also built by the Robin, Hedge-sparrow, Nightingale, the Thrush family, and a great many others. Sometimes we find them in the oddest places—in old kettles and buckets, in lamps and pumps and flower-pots *(see* picture *below)*, and even in the torn hat of a scarecrow!

ROBIN AND NEST IN FLOWER-POT

Another lovely nursery is that of the Chaffinch—a cup-shaped nest of moss, grass and wool, lined with hair and feathers, and the outside decorated with lichen. Built in the branches of an old apple tree, it needs sharp eyes to detect this elegant nursery.

Probably the Chaffinch does not use lichen for the purpose of hiding the nest. All birds like to use dead, dry stuff for building, and lichen is dry and papery. Sometimes the Chaffinches build in a church-yard yew tree, and then you may perhaps see their nursery decorated with coloured *confetti!* If you hang bits of coloured wool and string in your garden, birds may carry them off as building material. Nesting material is not chosen for *colour* but for *usefulness*.

Larger birds, as you will have noticed, do not, as a rule, use fine and soft building material. Look at the rough nest of twigs made by the Wood Pigeon and Turtle Dove. Someone has said that the Dove's nest is "two long sticks and one short one"! These birds, as you know, are affectionate and very devoted to their young. But they take such little pains over their nursery that the eggs or young can sometimes be seen from below, through the bottom of the nest. And the wonder is that the helpless babies do not fall over the edge or through the floor!

A surprising nursery is that of the Magpie, one of our most beautiful and interesting birds. It is built, as a rule, in the upper branches of a high tree. The nest is a tangle of briars and thorns, inside which is another mass of twigs and mud and fine roots. And not content with building this castle, the Magpies fence it around with sticks and more thorns, leaving an entrance on one side. To finish off, the building is roofed over with thorns and twigs.

Even if you live in a town, there are many bird-nurseries to be seen. Some birds rear their young without the shelter of a nursery; others lay their eggs in the most extraordinary places; we must look at one or

1. NEST OF WEAVER BIRD
2. NEST OF SCARLET WEAVER BIRD

two of them in our next lesson. In museums you can see wonderful nests from foreign lands—the close-woven tubes of the Weaver-birds, the leaves sewn together by the Indian Tailor-bird, and the downy, thimble-like nursery of the lovely Humming-bird. They give us an idea of the care and skill of the bird in preparing for the young:

> "No tool had he that wrought; no knife to cut,
> No nail to fix, no bodkin to insert,
> No glue to join; his little beak was all;
> And yet how neatly finished! What nice hand
> With every implement and means of art,
> Could make me such another?"

EXERCISES

1. Name two bird-nests you have examined. What materials were used?

2. Name four birds which nest in holes. Which of them plasters up the entrance?

3. Describe the Magpie's nest. Where would you look for it?

4. Describe the nests of the Dove and the Long-Tailed Tit.

CHAPTER V
NURSERIES IN BIRDLAND (CONTINUED)

MANY birds rear their families without shelter of any sort, sometimes in the most unexpected places! Our beautiful sea-birds seldom trouble to construct nurseries. They frequent rocky ledges, high cliffs, or shingly stretches of coast, swept by the rough sea winds. In such wild places, of what use to build a dainty nest? It would be blown into the sea, and the precious eggs scattered or smashed!

So most shore-birds are content with a mere hollow scratched in the sand or shingle. The Oystercatcher or Sea Pie is one of these; perhaps you have seen him—a handsome fellow, with bright red beak and legs, and black-and-white body.

A scrape or two in the sand or pebbles satisfies the pretty Oyster-catchers *(see* picture on next page). They may decorate it with a few little stones or shells: so long as the eggs are above the highest tide-mark, they are content.

NATURE'S NURSERIES

OYSTER-CATCHER COVERING EGGS

The beautiful birds known as Sea-Swallows or Terns are common near most seaside places. They are like graceful, dainty sea-gulls, but more active, and with the forked tail that gives them the name of Sea-Swallow. They have the habit of suddenly dropping into the water like stones, in pursuit of their prey. They think a little hollow in the beach makes a suitable nursery, and I fear they are less careful than the Oyster-catcher, for every year an extra high spring tide will sweep away hundreds of their eggs. It is amusing to see some of these Terns pretend to make a nest on the bare beach. They bring a few dry stalks of sea grass.—The first high wind blows this pretence at a nest away, and then they solemnly begin again.

If you have ever searched for the eggs of these birds which breed in open spaces, you will know how

NURSERIES IN BIRDLAND (CONTINUED)

difficult they are to discover. You may walk quite near and yet not see them, even though they lie on the beach with no covering of any kind. The reason is that they are speckled, spotted, and blotched so that they are hidden amid the stones.

The most careless in its nursery habits is that sea-bird known as the Guillemot, a black-and-white diving bird. You may not see this bird during your summer holidays, as it keeps to the open sea. But, in nesting-time, Guillemots come to certain parts of our coast, where they cluster on the ledges in tens of thousands. So near are they to one another that there is scarce room for a single new-comer to squeeze itself on to the ledge.

And it is these ledges of rock, high above the roaring waves, that the Guillemot prefers for a nesting site. Here, on the bare rock, she lays her one egg. It is a large one, and tapers nearly to a point at one end, so that it does not easily roll about. Yet many of these eggs *do* roll off the ledge and smash on the rocks far below. It happens in this way. When brooding her egg, the Guillemot moves it on to her feet, and then sits on it! This helps to warm the egg; but it is liable to be jerked right off the ledge if she flies away in a hurry!

The baby Guillemot must have a very uncomfortable nursery life. And how it ever reaches its real home, the sea, is a puzzle. It leaves the "nest" long before it can fly; and the sea rages several hundred feet down below! Do the parents carry their baby down, or does it bravely drop over the edge, and flutter down as best it can?

Let us look now at a nursery in the far-off deserts of Africa. Here the largest of living birds, the Ostrich, makes its home. Thousands of Ostriches are now reared on farms, and their eggs are often hatched, like those of our fowls, in incubators. Out in the desert the Ostrich makes a nest simply by kicking a slight hollow in the sand. This duty falls to Mr. Ostrich, the hen bird standing by as he tears up the sand with his powerful legs.

Very soon he has made a shallow pit, about a yard wide, with the loose sand banked round it—like the pits dug by children at the seaside. This done, the Ostrich is quite content with his nest-making, and his wives—he has more than one—begin to fill the "nest" with eggs.

These eggs, as you know, are very large, each one weighing about three-and-a-quarter pounds. The hen Ostrich will lay ten or fifteen of them, so you can imagine the pile that fills the sandy nest! Then begins the long wait—over forty days—until the chicks appear. In very warm places the Ostriches let the sunshine and burning hot sand warm their eggs. After sprinkling sand over them, to hide them and also to shield them from the sun, they go to seek food and water. But during the night Mr. Ostrich warms them with his body. They are then quite safe from prowling jackals and others

NURSERIES IN BIRDLAND (CONTINUED)

fond of eggs for supper. With a furious war-cry, like the roar of a lion, the Ostrich runs at great speed upon the intruder: he has been known to kill a man with one kick!

The baby Ostriches are not in the least like the father or mother. Their necks are short, with stripes like those of a tiger, and instead of the soft down worn by most chicks, these odd babies seem covered with spines, like two-legged hedgehogs.

As the egg is about thirty times the size of an ordinary hen's egg, you will not be surprised to know that these chicks are twelve inches high when they first appear. They lose no time, and may be seen running with part of the egg-shell still on their backs! They grow apace, every month adding at least a foot to their height, until, at six months, they are "grownups."

From the hot, sandy desert we will plunge into the very coldest, bleakest part of the earth, and there look at the most astonishing nursery of all. In the frozen wastes near the South Pole, where Jack Frost is king, and earth and sea are a mass of ice, the Emperor Penguin begins nursery duties. Few men have seen this peculiar bird in its dreadful home: at first people could scarcely believe the accounts of it told by brave explorers.

The Emperor Penguin lays its one egg at the very coldest time of year, during the polar winter, when dark night reigns, not for hours, but for months at a time! Terrible blinding snow-storms sweep across the

NATURE'S NURSERIES

1. GREAT SPOTTED WOODPECKER   2. SONG THRUSH
3. LONG-TAILED TIT   3. REED WARBLER'S NEST

ice-fields; and having nothing, not even a stone, for nesting material, this bird lays her egg upon the ice.

"The egg would freeze at once," you may say, "and be useless." That is true, and this odd bird gets over the difficulty in an odd way. She puts her feet under the egg as soon as it is laid. Then she lowers her body, and a large flap of skin folds over the egg to keep it snug even during the most bitter blizzards. The chick also nestles into this cosy nursery!

Not many of these chicks ever live to grow up. And the strange thing is that they die, not of cold, but of too much loving care! Let us see what happens, in

NURSERIES IN BIRDLAND (CONTINUED)

the words of an observer:

"All the adult Penguins long to nurse a chick of their own. One chick I noticed standing away from its mother for a moment. At once half a dozen chick-less adults bore down upon it, only to meet and struggle for its possession. The chick could not escape, and, of course, was trampled and clawed to death. The same scene occurred every time a chick wandered.

"The maternal instinct of the Emperor is so strong that even frozen and lifeless chicks are carried about and nursed until their down is worn away. Sometimes avalanches of ice and snow would drive the Emperor from its egg; but it always returns to the frozen egg, and will sit on it until it is rotten."

Of all bird-nurseries none is more surprising than this!

EXERCISES

1. Where would you look for the eggs of Tern, Oyster-catcher, and Guillemot?

2. Why do many sea-birds make such slight nests?

3. Write a story about Mr. Ostrich, his nest, eggs, and chicks.

CHAPTER VI
MEAL-TIME IN BIRDLAND

IN most birdland nurseries there is no breakfast-hour or dinner-time. The baby bird wants food; he *squeaks* or *cheeps* until he gets it, and not until he is satisfied does he cease to ask for more. Tap the edge of the nest, and up come all the hungry heads, with gaping beaks, as if worked by a spring *(see* picture *opposite)*. They think that mother or father has alighted with a beakful of food.

The parent bird, bringing home a grub, finds perhaps ten open mouths. They all want the choice morsel! How is she to know "whose turn" it is? The answer is, she does not worry about such matters. She fetches more and more food until every hungry mite is, for the time, quiet; then she takes a well-earned rest and a meal for herself.

Babies, all the world over, need special food, and soon die if they do not have that food and no other. Watch the House-Sparrows feeding their brood in their untidy nursery; or the Chaffinch with her beautiful nest in the apple tree. Both these birds love seeds. Nature gave them *hard* bills to deal with such food. But their babies have *soft* bills and soft stomachs, too, at first, quite unfitted to consume hard fare. So the parents bring for them grubs, worms, flies, and other tender tit-bits. They know by *instinct* which food is most suitable.

YOUNG THRUSHES—8 DAYS OLD

Insect-eating birds like the Swallow, Wagtail, Robin, and a great many others, have hard labour indeed to find meals for the nursery. Darting rapidly here and there, the Wagtail snaps up fly after fly until you may see a fringe of legs and wings round her beak. The Swallows and Martins pay many a visit to their nests, each time with a supply of insect food.

But the Swift, that living aeroplane, is more fortunate. His habit is to tear through the air with gaping mouth, fly-catching. If you could peep into the nest you would say he was a poor hunter, and had brought home no dinner for his two little ones. Then his bill opens wide. Like a conjurer, he produces scores of flies glued together into a mass as large as a marble. He had carried them under his tongue.

The Rook also "pouches" food for his noisy family, and so does the Bullfinch. This dodge saves many a journey, does it not? All the same, nesting-time is hard work, and long before the nestlings fly, the parent birds look worn and torn.

BABY HERONS—ONE WEEK OLD

No parent bird works harder than that fine fisherman, the long-billed Heron. Meal-time; in his nursery, seems to go on all day and all night. The young ones spy him as he flaps heavily to the big nest in the tree-top *(see* picture *above).* In their harsh voices they seem to shout, "Hurry up! Hurry up! We are starving!" He seems to have nothing to give them—but they know better. Father Heron opens his great bill, and one by one they plunge their own within it. What a mixed dish they find! An eel, a frog or two, some newts, fish, a young rat, and other trifles. "Not a very tempting dinner," you may say. But the ravenous young Herons soon make an end of it!

There are, as you know, many "patent" foods, as we call them, for human babies. Some feathered folk, too, use a special kind of baby-food. Perhaps you have watched the Pigeon feed her young. Hard grain would kill the newly-hatched Pigeon, so she provides for it special food, and feeds it in a special way. Taking its bill in her own, with an up-and-down movement she gives the nestling food prepared in her own *crop*. This food is rather like curdled milk in appearance. After some days it is less milky, being mixed with harder food. A few more days, and the young pigeon is ready for "grown-up" meals; but the hard grains are still made soft for it by the careful parents. In due course the youngster's big, soft beak shrinks and hardens, and it is able to pick up and digest grain for itself.

The nurseries we have peeped into at meal-time have all contained youngsters that are nearly helpless. The baby Sparrow, for instance, is a naked, blind little creature. It is very feeble, and droops weakly in the nest waiting for father or mother to keep it warm and to serve the next meal. Until its naked body has a coat of feathers, and its legs and wings are strong, it must stay at home. If it is too adventurous, it may fall *plop!* out of the nest and become a meal for the cat!

How different is this baby from the duckling or the barnyard chick! Soon after their backs are clear of the egg-shell these pretty mites want to see the world. No waiting in the nursery for them! Quick and alert, the chicks follow the old hen, who fusses over them and shows them what to eat. Very soon they begin to scratch for their own food. It is important that the young of those birds which nest on the ground should be able to run, and hide, and feed soon after leaving the egg. Baby Pheasants, Partridges, Plovers, Ostriches, and many others all behave in this way. Their nursery life is a hardy one, not at all like that of the baby Pigeon, Sparrow, Robin, and a host of others.

We must now visit the nests of some birds-of-prey at meal-time. Have you ever found the larder of that handsome fellow, the Red-backed Shrike? His nest is often to be found in a thorn bush, and the larder not far away. You may find beetles, bees, frogs, mice, or small birds all stuck on the thorns, which this bird uses as a butcher uses meat-hooks in his shop.

He tears the prey to pieces for his family, Mrs. Shrike being an even cleverer butcher than her husband! I have seen them catching fat bumblebees. These they stuck neatly on a barbed wire fence before carrying them off to the nursery in the hedgerow.

Birds-of-prey give their fierce-eyed children big meals—more, indeed, than they can eat! In the dark nursery of the Barn Owl there is often a huge supply of food. You may find there more than a dozen mice and young rats, all laid out in neat rows. More freshly-killed meat than the family can eat!

In nesting-time Barn Owls hunt farmyards and hedgerows eagerly for their prey. Like many other birds, they help the farmer while helping themselves. Every Barn Owl puts money in the farmer's pocket! And so we should encourage such birds as much as we can, and never by any chance molest them or their nurseries.

That terror of the small birds, the Sparrow Hawk, shares the duties of the nursery with his wife. The mother-bird tends the young while her mate hunts for food. Let us visit the woods, hide carefully, and watch their nest. Their babies are growing up, and now and again a white fluffy head, with curved beak and staring eyes, shows over the rim of the rough nest.

We hear a *swish* of wings and look up to see the male bird dart through the tree-tops. He does not fly to the nest, but perches high up, and we can see that he holds in his talons a bird the size of a thrush.

He has already plucked off most of its feathers. Baby Hawks live well, and we notice that the parents prepare their meals by removing the dry, choking feathers.

NATURE'S NURSERIES

But look! The Hawk swoops, drops his prey on the edge of the nest, and off he goes to hunt for more! The greedy babies squeak and struggle for the food. But the mother Hawk stands on it and pulls it to bits with her beak, and each youngster gets a share. One, larger than the rest, stands up to snatch a piece from the mother. She holds it away, and there is a tug-of-war until the food breaks, and each swallows a piece!

1. GREENFINCH   2. BULLFINCH   3. CHAFFINCH
4. YELLOW HAMMER   5. GOLDFINCH

In three minutes the meal is all over, and the nest is peaceful once more. The young are sleepy after their food. But, if you remain quite still, you will soon see the father Hawk return with another victim. Sometimes his mate goes a-hunting too. But, as a rule, he catches, kills, and plucks the prey, while the strong and fierce

MEAL-TIME IN BIRDLAND

mother-bird guards the home and serves out their meals to the downy nestlings whom she loves so well.

EXERCISES

1. Name some grain-eating birds that feed their young on soft food.

2. How does the Pigeon feed its young?

3. Describe how the Heron and the Sparrow Hawk feed their nestlings.

4. Watch birds feeding their young, and try to find out the kind of food each brings to the nest.

CHAPTER VII
LESSON-TIME IN BIRDLAND

Young birds begin life with some of their lessons already learned. In fact, they may know how to use their knowledge *even before they are hatched!* This sounds rather odd, does it not? But it is quite true, as you will see from this little story told by a well-known lover of birds:

"Finding the nest of a Moorhen, I saw that all the chicks but one were already hatched, and were hiding in the rushes with their mother. So I stood by the pond and watched this last chick opening his shell. (*See* picture *opposite.*)

"He was *cheeping* vigorously inside, and I could see the crack which he was cutting round the middle of the egg getting longer every second. At this moment the mother Moorhen came out of the rushes and, seeing me standing by her nest, uttered a sudden sharp cry of warning.

"On the instant, the little unhatched bird stopped his work and his *cheeping*. And, though I stayed for quite ten minutes, there was neither sound nor movement in the egg afterwards. So I went away and left the nest in peace."

YOUNG MOORHENS HATCHING OUT

Now this baby had never even set eyes on its parents. So. we cannot help asking: "How did it know the meaning of that danger signal?" No one can give us a complete answer to that question. All animals *know* certain things without having to learn them. Such knowledge is said to come by *instinct*. The call that means "food," and the call that spells "danger," and many other things too, are well understood by chicks. Let us say that this wonderful guide we call *instinct* is ready-made knowledge.

In the life of all Nature's children it plays a very important part. For instance, no one *taught* the baby Moorhen inside the egg that it must hammer with its beak in order to break the prison walls! It hammers away without knowing *why* it does so!

In the same way, the Moorhen chick needs no lessons in swimming. I once watched one leave the nest and enter the water. He was but a few hours old. And so weak was he that he could not walk properly: he used the tips of his tiny wings as crutches while he climbed over the rough nest. Yet, as soon as he reached the edge, he plopped boldly into the water, and paddled away into the unknown world of the pond with all his might. We see again that the baby bird knew *by instinct* the right thing to do.

Now the world is not a friendly place for babies that are good to eat—baby birds are on the dinner-list of many fierce enemies. Strangely enough, they seem at first unable to tell friend from foe. Here, then, is a lesson they *must* learn, for it means life or death. As the cat steals silently through the shrubbery thinking of tender chick for dinner, you hear perhaps the shrill call of the Robin, or the anxious warning cry of Mother Thrush, who has a fledged family to feed. At once the baby Thrushes squat down like frogs, and remain quite still, as if glued to the earth. Pussy may pass near by, but they remain motionless.

You may see the same thing as you wander over open fields, where there are happy families of Partridges. They see you long before you know they are there. A call from the old bird, and the family crouches down and remains perfectly still. There they stay, eight or nine little balls of speckled fluff, looking like clods of earth.

LESSON-TIME IN BIRDLAND

The danger signal is obeyed without a moment's pause.

Leaving this happy family, we glance at another one in the farmyard, where an old hen is proudly leading her dozen chicks, finding food for them. No one could call her a singer, but as a talker she beats most birds. She has many "call-notes." How well the chicks know that cluck which means, "Come along, here's something good to eat!" She breaks up the food, and even pretends to eat some herself. When they rush in their eager way to snap at something harmful, the fussy old hen gives loud warning. It is not long before they learn caution, and to distrust unknown things.

The barn-yard chicks are not the only ones that need lessons at feeding-time. A very different nursery scene takes places on a wild mountain-side of Scotland. Here that splendid bird, the Golden Eagle, has her nest or *eyrie*.

"The young Eagles," says a naturalist who watched the eyrie for many days, "were fed at first on dainty tit-bits. The old Eagles tore up hares, rabbits and grouse, and presented the livers only to the ravenous youngsters. Afterwards, I saw them take bits of flesh as well as the livers from the beak of the mother bird. Then, later on, she gave up this habit; she tore up her prey, ate part of it herself, and offered the rest to her young so that they could pick out morsels for themselves. This taught them they must learn to help themselves. A day or two after, they kept calling for food even when half a rabbit lay in the nest.

"This seemed to annoy the big Eagle. She ate part of it and flew away with the remainder! It seemed to be a punishment for laziness! However, in a few days I saw them with a whole rabbit, which they tore up and swallowed bones and all! Just as mother had done it!"

Few people ever see these interesting baby Eagles. But, if you know where to look, and how to keep still, you may watch other young birds at their feeding lessons. By the brook-side you may find Mr. and Mrs. Kingfisher with their charming family of seven or eight. They were born near by, on a heap of fish bones, in a dark hole in a clay bank. It was not a very pleasant kind of home, to our thinking. But they have left it now; and, seated in a row on a dead branch that overhangs the brook, they are squeaking for dinner, and bobbing up and down like queer little toys.

Now and again the old birds dart away to find food. But it is evident that they think it high time the family learnt to fish for themselves! For, instead of feeding the hungry ones, they sometimes drop a tiny dead fish or other tasty morsel in the shallow water near by. In this way do they encourage the babies to learn how to earn their daily food. It must be no easy matter to plunge into the water, as the Kingfisher does, and capture an active minnow.

Little birds use their wings by instinct. But they must practise before they learn all the secrets of the air. Some are slower than others at learning; so pussy, at this time of year, grows sleek and fat!

Baby Swallows seem to need no lessons. They boldly throw themselves from the nest and fly at once, easily and well. The babies of most water-birds, like the Duck and Moorhen, need no lessons in swimming. But the Dabchick or Little Grebe, which frequents many of our lakes and rivers, has been seen to dive with a young one tucked under its wing. As the baby is a perfect swimmer it comes to no harm.

Even the Penguin, which swims and dives like a fish, has to be sent into the water by force. These birds (which you may see at the Zoo) spend most of their time in the open sea; yet their young are at first afraid to enter the water. The old birds push them in; and in a few hours they are the champion divers of all the birds in the world!

EXERCISES

1. Tell in your own words the story of the baby Moorhen in this lesson.

2. In what ways do baby chicks show us that they perform many of their actions by instinct?

3. What lessons do the parent Kingfishers and Penguins give their young ones?

CHAPTER VIII

THE BABES IN THE WOOD

In this lesson let us peep into the nurseries of some of the woodland folk. As you know, the highest class of the animal kingdom is that of the *Mammals*, so called because the mother feeds her young with milk from her own body. As a rule, the babies appear in the world quite helpless. Their eyelids have not yet opened, and their weak little bodies are naked, or have but a thin coat of hairs.

Baby mammals, then, must have some sort of nursery life, until such time as they are fit to leave their parents and face the world on their own.

In this country there are not very many wild mammals. Rats and mice are the commonest, and next to them in numbers we should perhaps place the Rabbit. Few babies look more helpless than the newborn Rabbits. The *doe* hides them so well that we shall not easily discover her secret. We find plenty of ordinary burrows in the rabbit *warren*. But mother Bunny has left the warren, and sought a special place to dig her nursery. It is about two feet in length. The ordinary burrow has several doors, as a rule; the nursery has but one opening. The Rabbit suckles her young at night, and when she leaves them, is most careful to stop up the entrance with earth. Knowing this habit, game-keepers and others call her nursery a "stop."

YOUNG RABBITS

The babies are in a roundish room at the end of the "stop," snug and warm in a blanket of softest down plucked by the mother from her own body. In spite of all her secrecy and care, accidents occur. Mole, the busy miner, has a trick of digging his shaft near by, and munches baby bunny for dinner. The Fox and the Badger, once their keen noses have discovered the secret, lose no time in securing such a delicate meal!

Blind, naked and helpless as they are at first, it is surprising how rapidly these babies grow up! They soon peep out at the big world, and hop a few paces from home. Their nursery life is now nearly over. It is just as well that they can care for themselves, for mother Bunny very soon has a second family to think about.

Now it is strange to find how different is the nursery life of Bunny's long-legged cousin, the Hare. Hares, as you know, do not seek safety in deep burrows. They rely instead on their power of hiding from their enemies; and, once they are discovered, to escape by running at great speed, twisting and doubling to baffle their foe. The Hare runs in great leaps, and, as its hind legs are so much longer than the front ones, its speed is greater up-hill than down! Its large ears can be turned in any direction, to pick up the slightest sound; so it is well able to do without the shelter of a burrow.

Early in Spring, mother Hare begins her nursery duties, but she never attempts to hide her young in a "stop." If you happened to find them, you would notice at once how different they are from baby Rabbits. Instead of being blind and naked, their eyes are open, and they wear a *thick coat of fur!* Also, they are strong on their legs, and soon able to follow the mother. So it is not surprising, after all, that the Hare takes less trouble than the Rabbit over her nursery arrangements. For the *leverets,* as her babies are called, have a much better start in life. We might compare the young of Rabbits and Hares with those of Sparrows and Partridges. Those

THE BABES IN THE WOOD

babies with no nursery are given strength and fitness to face the world.

Very soon the leverets are able to take care of themselves, and to make their own beds. They squat in "forms" in the grass, keenly sifting the sounds with those long ears of theirs, and crouching motionless at the least hint of danger.

If you find the "form" where one of the leverets has rested in the spring herbage, you may tell by its size the age of the baby that made it. The mother Hare does not leave her young until they know the tricks that all Hares understand so well: to catch a Hare "napping" is rare indeed!

HARE CROUCHING IN FORM

HARE IN WINTER

THE BABES IN THE WOOD

Leaving the timid Hare crouching in her "form," we will look now at a very different kind of nursery—that of the fiercest animal still to be found in the British Isles. A long while ago great forests spread over our land, the home of many fierce creatures. As the land was cleared and became cultivated, these animals disappeared, one by one; we can still see them—and even their young—but only at the Zoo!

There is, however, one fierce *carnivore* or flesh-eater left, and that is the Wild Cat. A few, but only a few, of these savage beasts still hunt in the wildest parts of the Highlands of Scotland. In the dense forests of those lonely places are some that have found a refuge, where they live and hide their nurseries.

These Wild Cats are *not* domestic pussies that have "gone wild." As you see in our picture *(on the next page)*, the Wild Cat resembles a tame tabby cat. It is, however, a bigger animal, and you will notice that the tail, with its nine black rings, has no pointed tip. A few years ago a Wild Cat was shot that measured, from its nose to the end of its bushy tail, more than four feet!

Someone has called this cat the British Tiger. It well deserves the name, for no tiger could be more savage. For its size, it is one of the strongest creatures in the world: it is also brave, fearless, and a mighty hunter. Well it is for the farmer and poultry-keeper that these hunters and killers are not plentiful!

To rear its five or six kittens, the Wild Cat chooses

a cleft in the rocks or a hollow tree. Even the nest of a Crow, or the hole of a Badger, is said to be used at times. The kittens look like our own jolly little friends on the hearthrug, playful balls of fur. But woe betide the person who dares to touch them! If the mother is near she will not hesitate to attack; and from the very first the young are savage and fierce, ready to growl and spit and fight with tooth and claw! They belong to the wild, and cannot be tamed.

WILD CAT

When the kittens are old enough, the female Cat goes a-hunting for her savage nursery. She fetches mice, rats, birds and other small game. Like our own pussy, she is a very devoted mother, looking after her children until they are nearly half-grown. They learn to hunt for themselves then, to stalk and kill such prey

THE BABES IN THE WOOD

as rabbits, hares, rats, squirrels and birds. Needless to say, no enemy dare venture near the nursery of this bloodthirsty creature, the last of the savage beasts that once roamed our land.

EXERCISES

1. Explain these words: stop, warren, burrow, leveret, carnivore, mammal, form.

2. Compare the baby Rabbit with the baby Hare, and say what you know about their nurseries.

3. Where is the Wild Cat still to be found? What is it like?

CHAPTER IX

THE BABES IN THE WOOD (CONTINUED)

To find the nursery of Mr. and Mrs. Prickles, the Hedgehogs, you must search the tangled roots of hedgerow trees, and the holes in banks and old walls. It is quite a snug, comfortable sort of nursery, with a roof, and it is carefully made of dead leaves, grass, and perhaps a little moss. The Hedgehogs wisely choose the month of May for the business of bringing up a family. At that time the food they love—grubs, worms, snails, insects, eggs and young birds—is found in plenty. Mother Hedgehog must herself be well nourished in order to feed her four or five babies.

Odd-looking mites are these blind babies; at first you would be puzzled to name them! Their little bodies are covered with soft white hairs: later on, of course, these hairs will harden and become stiff spines.

The young Hedgehogs cannot roll themselves up into a tight ball until they are at least a month old. The happy family keep together, and it is some time before the young set out to face the world alone. They hide

THE BABES IN THE WOOD (CONTINUED)

away in hedgerow tangles. Your dog may smell them out and prick his nose, but otherwise you will not easily know their hiding-place.

At nightfall they are quite ready to set out on the quest for food. By autumn they are plump and well-fed, and prepare to sleep away the dreary months of winter in a nest like the one in which they were born. But not all of them! Foxes, badgers and dogs have been the death of some. And Mr. Gamekeeper will tell you how he kept missing eggs, night after night, until he set a trap to catch the thief, and found in it—a dead Hedgehog!

Another winter sleeper, the Dormouse, builds a modest little nursery, but not until Spring sunshine warms the earth. Her family are at first dressed in a mouse-grey colour, which, later on, turns to a pretty red-brown. In their winter sleep these Dormice look like fat lumps of laziness. But see them—if you can! — running and leaping in the hedgerow at dusk, and you will say that they look much more like little Squirrels than mice!

Harvest Mice build a nursery with neither front nor back door. One wonders how they manage to get in and out! And when the eight or nine wee babies are growing up, and quite fill the nest, it is another puzzle to know how the mother gets inside to feed them all!

Their nest is nearly ball-shaped, built of grass-blades woven together. The nimble little builders split the grass into shreds before plaiting it, and so well is the dainty nursery constructed that you can roll it about without spoiling it. The mice use three or four grass-stems or corn-stalks as scaffolding.

This sounds a frail support for a home: but the Harvest Mouse is one of the smallest mammals in the world. It is nearly the same weight as a halfpenny! It can easily climb a wheat-stalk and feast on the corn in the ear *(see* picture *opposite)*. There is no prettier sight than a party of these little mice darting up, and down, in and out the stalks, sometimes pausing to nibble at the corn, sometimes darting on an unwary bluebottle. In the autumn they, too, seek a sleeping-place; they first gather a store of food, being light sleepers!

The Squirrel builds two kinds of nests, or dreys as they are called: one is for the babies, the other, built in the trees by both Mr. and Mrs. Squirrel, is a living-place, made of moss, leaves, twigs, and shreds of bark *(see* coloured picture, page 62). If the nest is easily seen, you may be sure it is not a nursery, for that is always hidden, perhaps in a holly or other evergreen; the Squirrel prepares early in the year for her family, before the leaves have burst their overcoats.

She will never enter her nest until she is quite certain the "coast is clear." Her three or four babies, so naked and helpless-looking at first, take lessons in climbing when a few weeks old: they follow their mother, who rewards them with morsels of food. Thus they learn to leap surely and well, from one swaying twig to another, and to know the paths through the tree-tops. These lessons and games continue for about six weeks.

THE HARVEST MOUSE

A very different nursery is that of Mole the Miner. Spring-time, when birds are singing and the woods and hedges at their gayest, is fighting-time for Mr. Mole. He is then ready to "go for" any other "gentleman in velvet" he happens to meet. His quarrels always end in a fierce fight, the fight may end in the death of one of the fighters, and the winner is ready to feast on the body of his beaten foe!

Meanwhile, Mrs. Mole is busy digging out a large room for her nest, which is a round mass of leaves and dried grass. The blind babies are pinkish in colour, and scarce longer than your little finger (*see* picture on page 63). Moles, as you know, earn their daily food by

SQUIRREL PREPARING HIS DREY

THE BABES IN THE WOOD (CONTINUED)

digging: so the young do not start life on their own until their bodies are fit to undertake such very hard work!

YOUNG MOLES

Perhaps it is hard work that gives this miner his splendid appetite. Moles are always ready for dinner, and never know when to stop! A captive Mole was found to eat, in three days: "Three or four dozen earthworms, a large frog, a quantity of raw beef, the body of a turkey-poult and part of a second, as well as one or two black slugs!" A boy with such an appetite would consume a whole sheep for dinner, and then feel hungry!

The strangest nursery-life is that of the Bat—the odd little beast whom so few people understand. Indeed, there are still some who say it is a bird with wings of skin!

NATURE'S NURSERIES

"What shall I call thee—bird or beast or neither?
Just what you will—I'm rather both than either:
Much like the season when I whirl my flight,
The dusk of evening—neither day nor night."

As she spends her life flitting through the air or hanging upside-down in a dark corner, the mother Bat has to carry her young one with her. So it digs its tiny claws into her soft fur, and clings close as she dives and twists in the air. Being a mammal, she feeds it as all baby mammals are fed. To us it seems a hideous, blind, skinny, naked little object!

The common Bat is known as the *Pipistrelle*. That larger one, flitting higher in the air, is the *Noctule*. It has a wrinkled face, with deep-set eyes, like an ugly little bull-dog, and its baby is even uglier!

EXERCISES

1. Describe the nursery of the Hedgehog. Where would you look for it?

2. Write a little story about the Harvest Mouse, its nursery, and young ones.

3. What is a drey? Why does the Squirrel often choose an evergreen tree in which to build her nursery?

4. Name two kinds of Bat.

CHAPTER X

BEWARE OF THE ENEMY!

FEW of our wild birds and animals die of old age. Besides the risks they run from bad weather and starvation, most of them have deadly foes. And no time is so full of danger as nursery-time, both for the young ones and their parents. It is a game of hide-and-seek in which the losers pay with their lives!

Hidden away in wood, field, and hedgerow are many nurseries of helpless little ones. Some, of course, are much quicker than others in growing up and looking after themselves. But, until that time, all of them depend on the cunning and the courage of their parents to save them from death. As we must find time in this lesson to see how our bird friends play this game of hide-and seek, we can glance at one wild animal only. Let us see how the timid Hare tries to baffle her foes and protect her nursery.

She is rightly known as a timid, nervous animal, always ready to run away at top speed. As she crouches in her "form" she looks the picture of dread. But an astonishing change comes over her if danger threatens her precious young. Forgetting to be timid, she defends them with her life. Even her cousin, the Rabbit, a weak and rather stupid creature, plucks up courage when she has a family to defend. As a rule, she goes in the utmost terror of the bloodthirsty Stoat, and gives up her life without the slightest attempt to struggle. But, when the Stoat attacks her nursery, she has been seen to give him the surprise of his life!

It is the same with all mothers! I once saw a cat running from an angry mother Blackbird which was dashing at it and pecking hard! We may think baby Blackbirds ugly, naked, little sprawlers. Or, if we peep into many another nursery, we may wonder at all the care and love given to such strange-looking objects! But the parent bird or animal thinks—otherwise!

Let us return to the mother Hare. She is well aware of the prowling, hungry foes all too eager to find her nursery in the open fields. She knows, too, that her babies are not yet ready to trust to their long legs if attacked. So she artfully hides each *leveret* in a separate place, making a little hollow or "form" for it, and concealing it in the grass with all her skill. There the babies crouch in hiding. This dodge, making several nurseries instead of one, often saves the life of her young. She is very attentive to them, visiting each leveret in turn at mealtimes.

Another trick of hers is also interesting. Knowing that her visits may attract the notice of the enemy, she is

BEWARE OF THE ENEMY!

at great pains to conceal her tracks. She will run this way and that, making a criss-cross track rather than give the game away by making a direct path! And she will keep away as long as a foe is lurking near. Mr. Hare leaves to her all the nursery work as well as the education of the little leverets.

Let us glance now at the feathered folk. Though the nursery may be well hidden from wind and weather, the dreaded Weasel can squeeze into the tiniest hole! In the game of hide-and-seek he is a clever seeker. For that purpose his body is lithe and strong, his nose keen, his teeth sharp and cruel.

Jays, Crows, Magpies and Squirrels are also well aware that eggs and young birds are good food. Another daring egg-thief is the Rat; he will even rob the hen-roost and, in a secret way of his own, will carry a big egg, weighing two ounces, out of the hen-house, down the ladder, and along the ground to his hole!

Such enemies as those empty many a nursery. When the young birds are squeaking for "Food! More food!" all day long, and the old birds must visit the nest frequently, the danger is greater still. When the fledglings have left the nursery, you may hear loud cries of alarm from many an anxious parent. It tells you that a fierce Stoat is hunting in the hedgerow, or a prowling cat is on the trail, knowing that the shrubbery hides fat young Thrushes or Blackbirds. There are enemies even in the air, where the swift Sparrow-Hawk pounces with sharp, curved talons.

This game of hide-and-seek may seem to us a very cruel one. But we must not forget that the *seekers* have a useful part in the plan of Nature. If *all* baby birds lived to grow up and start nurseries of their own, what would happen? Mrs. Sparrow has a family of about five babies three times a year. These fifteen little Sparrows would soon grow up and begin to build nests. We need not be very clever at arithmetic to reckon how soon, at that rate, our gardens would be packed with thousands and thousands of Sparrows. And then a famine would result, and all would die of hunger and disease.

Out in the open, young birds are more artful than those of the hedgerow. As every Scout knows, it is fatal to show yourself to the enemy above ground-level, with the sky as background! So the baby Partridges, Grouse, Plovers, and other birds of the open, crouch to the earth as you approach them. They know *by instinct* that that is the wisest thing to do!

Another dodge which some birds practise by instinct is stranger still. As you approach the family party, the parent leaves the young, and flies or runs slowly away. Then you notice that the poor bird is badly hurt. Perhaps a wing droops sadly down, or one leg trails behind the other. The bird shuffles along with pain, and then almost lies down, unable to move a step farther.

But a minute later the "wounded" bird flies

BEWARE OF THE ENEMY!

swiftly up, having drawn you safely away from the spot where her brood is in hiding. Ducks, Plovers, and Partridges are clever at this dodge; and I have seen even the little Willow Wren act in this way. Weak birds must employ such tricks to guard their young from danger: few are able to use sheer strength like the great Ostrich, which, with one kick, can slay the creature rash enough to inquire too closely into his nursery arrangements!

EXERCISES

1. Write a story about the Hare, and how she tries to save the leverets from danger.

2. What enemies must the parent birds guard against?

3. How do baby Partridges try to escape their enemies? Describe how some birds lure their enemies away from the young.

CHAPTER XI

PLAYTIME

NESTING-TIME is a serious business, and then there is no time for frolics. But, as soon as family cares are over, both young birds and old may join in the games they prefer; some of them seem to enjoy playing as much as boys and girls.

All sorts of games are played in bird-land—and mischief enters into some of them! A Cockatoo escaped from the large open-air cage at the Zoo, and after a day or two spent happily in the tree-tops, he was recaptured. But having learnt the trick of escaping, he was soon free again. This time he refused to enter the traps set for him by the keepers, and decided to enjoy his liberty. Not only that, but for fun and mischief he attacked the wires of the cage from the outside, and helped several of his friends to escape too! As soon as they were caught he repeated the game, much to the annoyance of the keepers, and they never succeeded in catching him alive!

Birds, like other creatures, vary in their love of play, and their skill in playing. The cleverest and most amusing are the Parrots, Cockatoos, and all the members of the Crow family. Parrots and Crows seem to think it fine fun to invent games and tricks. A Parrot who disliked a cat would imitate the plaintive *miauw* of a lost kitten. Then, when the cat ran to look for its little one, Polly would shriek with laughter.

A tame Raven—which, as you may know, is our largest member of the Crow family—invented another kind of teasing game. This bird disliked a certain dog, which had often dug up and eaten bones the Raven had hidden away. "The Raven," says someone who watched the fun, "would wait until the dog was curled up and asleep, then he would carefully drop a stick so as to annoy and awaken him. Well pleased at the result, the Raven would turn his head on one side in a wicked way, and give a hoarse chuckle as if he quite enjoyed the joke!"

Young Moorhens spend part of their time in "minding the baby." I do not know if we should call this play, but they seem to enjoy doing it. Mother Moorhen has several families every summer, so the babies of the first brood are very young when she turns them from the nest. They help to feed the youngsters of the second brood, and may even build rough nests for them. Nest-building and "minding the baby" are both useful pastimes, like many of the games of wild creatures.

In talking of the playfulness of birds, we must not omit that remarkable little fellow the Penguin. This is not the Emperor Penguin whom we met in Lesson V, but a smaller cousin, also to be found in the frozen South. Travellers in that terrible region tell us how fond of play are these gentle birds.

"No matter how miserable we felt," wrote one brave explorer, "but the sight of those jolly little birds cheered us up. They would crowd up to the very edge of the ice, dodging about and trying to push one another into the sea. Sometimes those behind would nearly succeed in pushing the front rank in, who then would just recover themselves in time, and rushing round to the rear try to turn the tables on the others.

"Sometimes one would really get pushed in, only to turn quickly under water and bound out again on to the ice, like a cork shot out of a bottle. They would chase one another about, bent on having a good game. Then, suddenly, each would take a header into the sea, and start splashing in the water and making sounds exactly like a lot of boys calling out and chaffing one another. They would also spend hours in playing at a sort of 'touch last' on the sea ice near the water's edge."

Games like that are played because the Penguins have nothing serious to do, and because they, like most of us, love doing things that don't "have to" be done.

But such games are of great use, for there comes a time when diving fast, and swimming well, and dodging in the water are most important. These little Penguins, for instance, have a terrible enemy, the Sea Leopard: it lies in wait for them near the edge of the ice floe. As soon as they enter the water a deadly chase begins, and a weak or slow Penguin is speedily caught and eaten by the monster.

Those swimming-games are therefore of value in the life of the bird: so, too, are the games of flying and fighting at which young birds love to play. Games of flying are often played by Rooks and Jackdaws, especially on a rough day. Then you may see them take wing and have rare fun as they balance against the wind over the tree-tops, swooping down and rising once more, and skilfully balancing against the gale. Another place for this kind of game is a steep cliff. A steady wind blows up the face of the cliff, and here you see a party of young Jackdaws at play. The rule seems to be that each bird must balance in the air at the top of the cliff without flapping a wing. They poise for as long as they can, and then shoot through the air and swing back into position once more.

Another bird of the Crow family actually makes a playground for itself. Indeed, there are several birds with this habit, but the one we know best is the handsome Bower Bird, for it sometimes builds its play-place, or bower, in our Zoo. Perhaps you know that the bower is built of twigs, arched over at the top: the floor is also of twigs, twisted and woven together, into which the ends of the twigs that form the walls are firmly fixed.

The Bower Birds' next task is to decorate their

playground; so they gather bones, feathers, leaves, flowers, and any bright object they can steal. These things are all brought to the bower, which then looks so odd that you would never guess it was the work of a bird.

As we have said, the Bower Bird is a foreign cousin of our own Rooks, Crows, Magpies and Jackdaws, who also love to pick up and carry away bright objects. The bower of the Bower Bird is built for fun and pleasure: it has nothing to do with the nest, which is a very ordinary building, like most of those constructed by members of the Crow tribe.

EXERCISES

1. Describe any games you have seen played by tame or wild birds.

2. Which birds often play at "minding the baby"?

3. Describe the games played by the Penguins. Of what use are such games to the bird?

CHAPTER XII
PLAYTIME (CONTINUED)

WHAT a jolly game the lambs are having in the fields! The serious business of feeding is over. The old ewes lie down and do nothing but look solemn and chew. But that is too slow for the lambs! Some of them still stand by their mammas, but the more playful ones are out for mischief. They rush at the quiet ones and butt them in the ribs!

This at once starts the merry game of running, butting and jumping. The good little lambs suddenly begin to jump around with legs as stiff as pokers. And then the dancing mob dashes at full speed up the field. Some of them rudely jump over the backs of their sleepy mothers! Then they join in a game of hop, skip, and jump, and a dozen of them run to a mound in the corner of the field.

A new game begins. (It is really that very old game called "Tom Tiddler's Ground.") In this game several lambs rush to the top of the mound, where there is room for one only. They jostle and push one another, and come helter-skelter down—but always on their feet!

Two of them collide and at once start a butting match. Others spring in the air with astonishing force, and fight enemies that do not exist! So the jolly romp goes on until all are tired.

Another pretty game might be seen in the coppice, where mother Fox is having some fun with her plump, snub-nosed little ones. She lies on her back, and they pretend they have found a dead bunny, and pull her about, even tugging at her tail. Mr. Fox, if he is at home, looks on, but pretends to be thinking of something else! The cubs love to toss a plaything in the air—a piece of wood, a dead bird, or any other toy!

They chase one another, bury the toy, and have great fun digging it up again! And all the while the vixen watches her babies, as they snap and snarl, and tumble in a happy heap in the sunshine. At the least hint of danger the cubs listen *(see* picture *opposite),* ready to disappear at once into the shelter of their hole.

In Chapter VIII we glanced at the nursery of the fiercest of all our wild mammals—the scarce Wild Cat, *(see* picture, page 56). Though its kittens are so fierce that they cannot be tamed, we are told that they romp and play with one another as merrily as our own domestic kittens. Few people ever see Wild Cats in their native home. As these creatures will soon disappear for ever from our land, it is interesting to read such stories of their home life as the following:

"I scrambled near the place chosen by the Cat for

PLAYTIME (CONTINUED)

her lair—a deep recess under some roots in the most secluded part of the hill-side. Through my glasses I was able to see the entrance quite plainly, and knowing that she had kittens hidden away, I waited in the hope of seeing them.

FOX CUB

"After some time . . . the fierce-looking Cat appeared, and to my delight she was followed by three handsome kittens. One after the other they climbed over the roots, and they were full of fun. Evidently the family was well fed, for, when one found a dead mouse it was used as a plaything and tossed here and there by those pretty, frolicsome balls of fur. The mother cat took no part in the games . . . and soon disappeared, no doubt to hunt for birds and mice for the larder!"

NATURE'S NURSERIES

All the big wild cousins of our cat have a love of play. Lion cubs have a long nursery life, following the lioness until they are nearly full-grown; they are always ready for play. Sometimes you may see baby Tigers, Lions, Leopards, and Jaguars at the Zoo. To keep them healthy and happy they are given playthings, such as large wooden balls. Their games are like those of the kitten, leaping at a rolling ball, patting it to this side and that, pretending to lose sight of it, and pouncing on it with a fierce spring!

Such games prepare these cats for the life they will lead as "grown-ups." Cats, big and little, hunt alone as a rule, and not in packs like most members of the dog tribe. The "stalking" and killing of game demand keen senses, and muscles as true as steel for the final pounce! So we are not surprised that their youthful games, though full of fun, are yet games of chase. A dead leaf or a wooden ball is stalked and "killed" with all the care and skill at the command of the growing kitten!

A rare sight is the playing and leaping of young Deer. In some of our parks you may see Fallow Deer and their *fawns;* and, less often, the large, stately Red Deer and their *calves.* In early summer the young are hidden away, but later on they practise leaping and running, in most delightful games. It is said that we owe the Fallow Deer to the *Romans.* In the New Forest these lovely Deer have always run quite wild, and there you may still see a scattered few.

PLAYTIME (CONTINUED)

In the same forest are also numbers of shaggy "New Forest Ponies." The playful antics of their long-legged colts are amusing to watch; like all colts, they seem to have legs several sizes too large for them! Soon enough, these babies have to settle down to the serious business of finding a living in the rough heather and sparse grassy patches of their home. Roaming as they please over the wide forest, no one tends or feeds these half-wild Ponies. Once a year all the colts are "rounded up" *(see* coloured picture *below)*.

COLT HUNTING IN THE NEW FOREST

Some animals, though playful when young, grow up to be quiet and sedate; others never lose their sense of fun. Of these we may mention the Otter, one of the most playful of animals. When meal-time is over, the Otter family play and sport in the water. Sometimes the clay bank of the stream is marked deeply where the merry party has played at "slides." They "follow my leader" down the bank, into the water, and up again.

Strange to say, even those deadly hunters, the Stoat and Weasel, are at times fond of a romp. Here is an account of a game played by a foreign cousin of our Weasel:

"They were the common larger kind of Weasel, about the size of a cat, and playing a performance that suggested dancing; they were so much taken up by their game that they did not notice me when I came within a few paces of them to see what they were doing. It proved to be a game of chase, played on a mound; they all, about a dozen in number, ran swiftly across, jumping over one another, turned at the end of the mound, and came flying back. Though full of excitement, they never collided. It was all done so quickly, and with such constant change of direction, that I could not follow a single animal with my eye, however hard I tried."

If you have ever watched a rabbit warren on a summer evening you will know how Bunny loves a game. Young and old join in a mad scamper, leap in the air, and run about as if playing at "touch." Watching them at their games, I am reminded of the clowns in a circus ring! Most animals seem to indulge in romps and fun as part of their lives—they believe that "all work and no play makes Jack a dull boy."

Like ourselves, they play because they enjoy it; but their games are not without meaning. The kitten's frolics prepare it for its life as a deadly hunter. The leaping lambs are learning to be strong, swift, and surefooted. The sheep of lowland pastures seem tame, slow,

PLAYTIME (CONTINUED)

silly creatures. But we must remember that all sheep come of a wild race whose home was the steep, rocky side of hill and mountain.

When the wolf or other enemy gave chase, the wild sheep ran for their lives. They leaped from rock to rock and ledge to ledge. Then only the active, strong, and sure-footed ones had any chance to escape the deadly foe behind them. The others were speedily eaten. So those early romps were part of their training, preparing their muscles and sinews, their eyes and feet for the deadly moment, when a swift run and a sure jump meant life or death!

EXERCISES

1. Describe the romps of the Lambs and Fox cubs.

2. Tell a story of a kitten and its play. Of what use are the romps of the kitten, and the lamb?

www.ingramcontent.com/pod-product-compliance
Lightning Source LLC
Chambersburg PA
CBHW042310150426
43198CB00001B/25